BOOK OF WONDERS
ACTIVITY BOOK

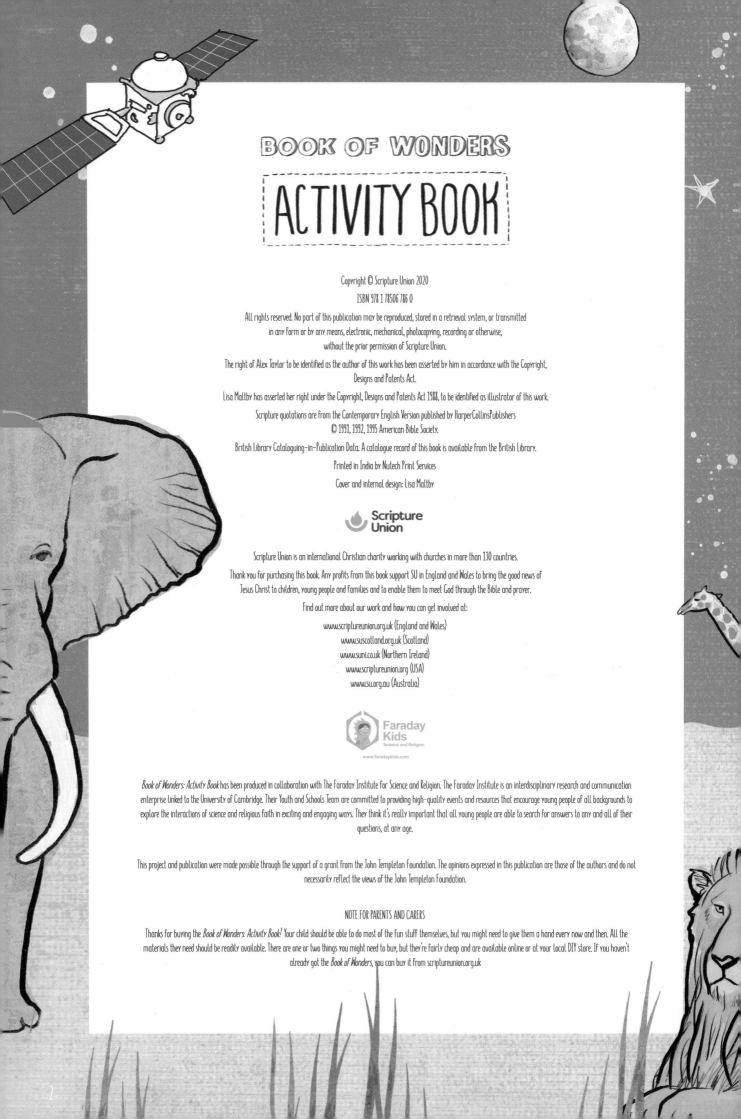

BOOK OF WONDERS

ACTIVITY BOOK

Printed in India by Nutech Print Services

Cover and internal design: Lisa Maltby

Scripture Union

Scripture Union is an international Christian charity working with churches in more than 130 countries.

Thank you for purchasing this book. Any profits from this book support SU in England and Wales to bring the good news of Jesus Christ to children, young people and families and to enable them to meet God through the Bible and prayer.

Find out more about our work and how you can get involved at:

www.scriptureunion.org.uk (England and Wales)
www.suscotland.org.uk (Scotland)
www.suni.co.uk (Northern Ireland)
www.scriptureunion.org (USA)
www.su.org.au (Australia)

Faraday Kids
Science and Religion
www.faradaykids.com

Book of Wonders: Activity Book has been produced in collaboration with The Faraday Institute for Science and Religion. The Faraday Institute is an interdisciplinary research and communication enterprise linked to the University of Cambridge. Their Youth and Schools Team are committed to providing high-quality events and resources that encourage young people of all backgrounds to explore the interactions of science and religious faith in exciting and engaging ways. They think it's really important that all young people are able to search for answers to any and all of their questions, at any age.

This project and publication were made possible through the support of a grant from the John Templeton Foundation. The opinions expressed in this publication are those of the authors and do not necessarily reflect the views of the John Templeton Foundation.

NOTE FOR PARENTS AND CARERS

Thanks for buying the Book of Wonders: Activity Book! Your child should be able to do most of the fun stuff themselves, but you might need to give them a hand every now and then. All the materials they need should be readily available. There are one or two things you might need to buy, but they're fairly cheap and are available online or at your local DIY store. If you haven't already got the Book of Wonders, you can buy it from scriptureunion.org.uk

WELCOME TO THE BOOK OF WONDERS: ACTIVITY BOOK!

HERE'S WHAT YOU'LL FIND INSIDE...

WELCOME TO YOUR BOOK

Congratulations on getting your hands on the *Book of Wonders: Activity Book!* You're holding a world full of discovery and wonder. Each page will help you explore yourself, the world around you, the planet you live on and the whole wide universe!

You can explore the book in whatever way you like – start at the beginning and work your way through, start at the end and go backwards or just open the book on any page and start there. The activities and experiments in the book are organised in four sections: About me, About my neighbourhood, About my world and About the universe. You could choose a section and do everything in that part of the book (The pages are colour coded to help you!).

For some of the activities, you'll need extra equipment or extra help. So make sure you've got a handy adult nearby who can work with you.

Use this book with the *Book of Wonders* so you can find out the most you can about the world around you and the God who made everything. Like the *Book of Wonders*, this activity book will also help you discover more about creator God and the fact that he wants to be your friend. Find out more on page 70.

Faraday
Kids
Science and Religion
www.faradaykids.com

If you want to explore more about science, faith, big questions and how those things can fit together, then go to the Faraday Kids site. You'll find lots of activities, features, videos and stories: faradaykids.com

ABOUT ME

You are an amazing creation! Yes, you are!
Fill this page with amazing facts about yourself.

Draw a self portrait

Name: ....

Age: ....

Gender: ....

Height: ....

Eye colour: ....

Hair colour: ....

Length of left leg: ....

Shoe size: ....

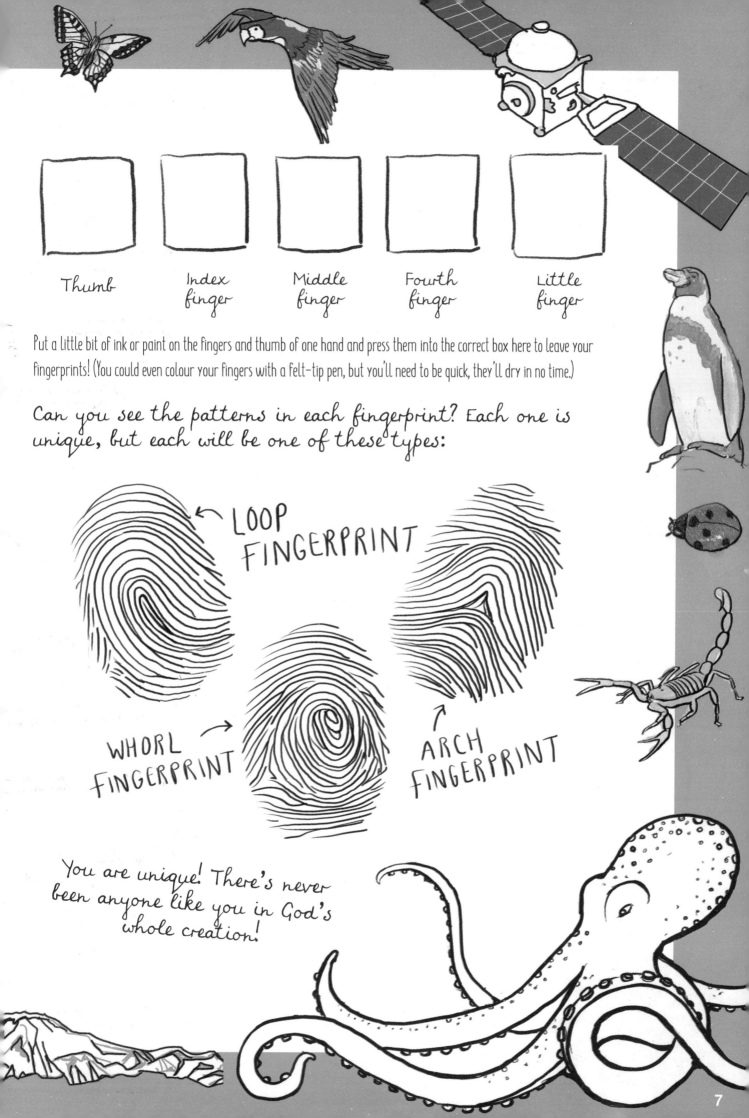

Thumb	Index finger	Middle finger	Fourth finger	Little finger

Put a little bit of ink or paint on the fingers and thumb of one hand and press them into the correct box here to leave your fingerprints! (You could even colour your fingers with a felt-tip pen, but you'll need to be quick, they'll dry in no time.)

Can you see the patterns in each fingerprint? Each one is unique, but each will be one of these types:

← LOOP FINGERPRINT

WHORL FINGERPRINT →

ARCH FINGERPRINT ↑

You are unique! There's never been anyone like you in God's whole creation!

WHAT ARE YOU MADE OF?

God made our bodies amazing! They are made of trillions of tiny bits called cells, too tiny to see. You have over 200 different types in your body doing over 200 different jobs!

Some cells help us see, some help us touch, some carry oxygen around, some help us digest food and some cells help us think.

Inside nearly every cell is a special set of instructions called DNA which tells the cell what its job is going to be and helps it make the equipment to do it. The bits of equipment that DNA helps cells to build are called proteins. They are like long chemical 'necklaces' made out of smaller chemical 'beads' called amino acids.

DNA looks like a twisted ladder with steps made from pairs of special chemicals called bases.

THERE ARE FOUR TYPES:

ADENINE (A)
CYTOSINE (C)
GUANINE (G)
THYMINE (T)

The DNA bases always pair up in specific ways:
Adenine (A) always pairs with Thymine (T).
Guanine (G) always pairs with Cytosine (C).

The order in which the bases are lined up along one side of the DNA is like a code, telling the cells what their job is. Each set of three DNA bases spell out a 'code word' which tells the cell which amino acid to put next in the protein necklace. Lots of the variety of God's creation comes from the different combinations of this clever DNA stuff.

We've created a chart with a letter of the alphabet* next to each amino acid, together with the sequence of DNA bases needed to make it. With just four colours of beads (like the four DNA bases) you can spell out your name or a message in the DNA code for those letters.

* There are only 20 amino acids in the genetic code and 26 letters in the alphabet, so we've had to make up the codes for some letters!

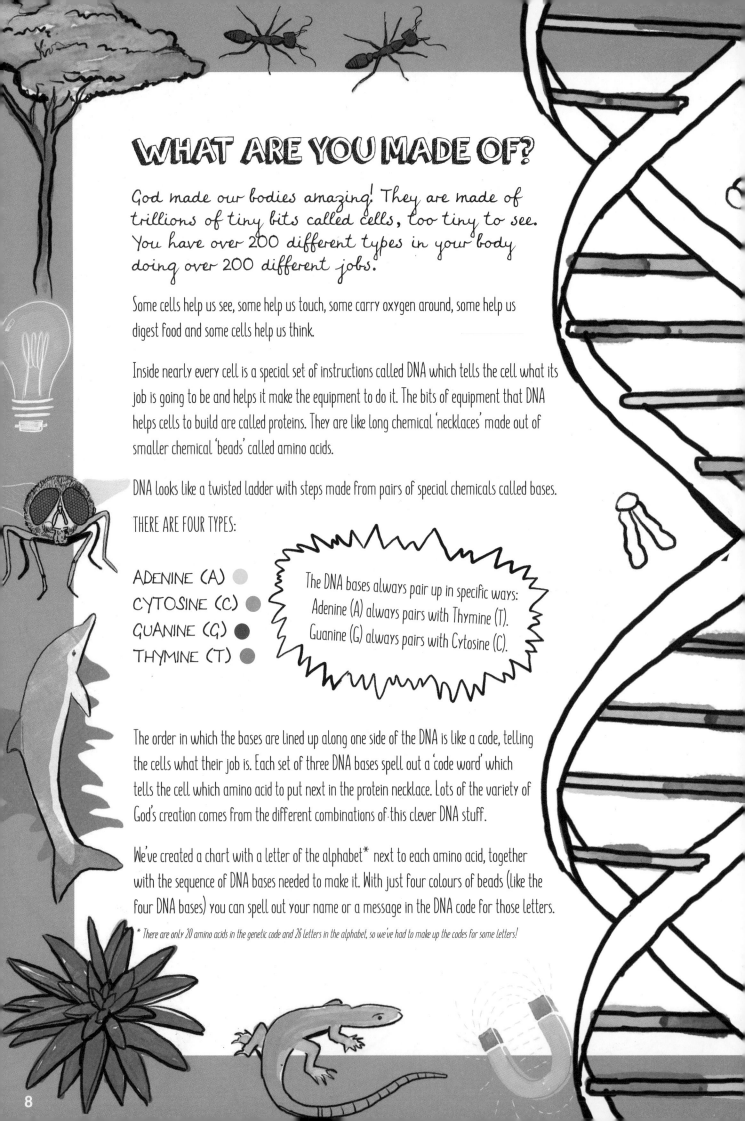

MAKE YOUR OWN DNA MESSAGE

YOU WILL NEED:

Elastic; coloured beads (for the bases) – red, blue, green, yellow

1. Choose a name or message to spell out (eg "Hello").
2. Look at the chart to find out the code for your first letter (eg H – blue, yellow, green).
3. Tie a knot in one end of your elastic (big enough to stop the beads falling off) and thread on the beads for your first letter.
   Repeat for each of your other letters. When you've finished, tie a knot in the other end and ask someone to help you tie the ends together.
   Wear your coded DNA message or give it to someone (with this chart) to see if they can work out what it says!

AMINO ACID	CODE	AMINO ACID	CODE
A Alanine	●●●	N Asparagine	●●●
B None	●●●	O None	●●●
C Cysteine	●●●	P Proline	●●●
D Aspartic acid	●●●	Q Glutamine	●●●
E Glutamic acid	●●●	R Arginine	●●●
F Phenylalanine	●●●	S Serine	●●●
G Glycine	●●●	T Threonine	●●●
H Histidine	●●●	U None	●●●
I Isoleucine	●●●	V Valine	●●●
J None	●●●	W Tryptophan	●●●
K Lysine	●●●	X None	●●●
L Leucine	●●●	Y Tyrosine	●●●
M Methionine	●●●	Z None	●●●

Why not find out what some of these amino acids do?

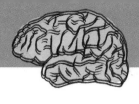

SET YOUR PERSONAL BEST

The way your body works is amazing! Use the *Book of Wonders* to find out all about your skeleton (page 90), your muscles (page 94), your eyes (page 40) and your sense of proprioception (page 47). Then use your bones, muscles, tendons, lungs, eyes and balance to set your personal bests.

How far can you jump?

Draw a line on the floor (or use some masking tape). Stand behind the line and jump forward as far as you can with your feet together. Then measure how far you jump. Do this three times and write your scores here:

Attempt 1: _____

Attempt 2: _____

Attempt 3: _____

Which was your best? _____

Can you keep a ball up?

Get a ball and kick it up in the air. How many times can you use your feet, knees, shoulders or head to keep the ball in the air? Try it three times and write your scores here:

Attempt 1: _____

Attempt 2: _____

Attempt 3: _____

Which was your best? _____

How good is your aim?

Find a small ball (like a ping-pong ball) and a mug. Put the mug on a table about a metre away from you. Can you throw the ball into the mug? Throw the ball towards the mug ten times. How many times did you succeed? Write that down next to 'Attempt 1', then do it twice more:

Attempt 1: _____

Attempt 2: _____

Attempt 3: _____

Which was your best? _____

How long can you balance for?

Find a stopwatch (or use the stopwatch app on a phone). Stand on one leg and time how long you can stand like this without putting both feet on the floor. Do this three times and write your scores here:

Attempt 1: ....

Attempt 2: ....

Attempt 3: ....

Which was your best? Are you better at standing on one leg than the other? ....

Can you score a goal?

You've seen penalty shoot-outs on TV, but can you score a penalty? Mark a goal at one end of your garden or in a park. Stand 5 m away and kick a football into your goal. How many can you score out of five? Try this three times and record your results here:

Attempt 1: ....

Attempt 2: ....

Attempt 3: ....

Which was your best? ....

(Make this harder by getting someone to be the goalkeeper!)

In all these activities, you use your body and your senses together. Isn't it wonderful how God made us all? God doesn't ask us to be as good at everything as other people, he asks us to use our gifts to be the best that we can be. That's part of what it means for us to be unique, and all loved by God.

TASTE SENSATION

What's your favourite food? Ask the people around you and record their answers in this table. Start with yourself!

Name	Favourite food	Sweet or savoury	Why

What percentage of people like sweet food best?
Find out by doing this calculation:

NUMBER OF PEOPLE WHO LIKE SWEET FOOD ÷ TOTAL NUMBER OF PEOPLE IN YOUR SURVEY x 100

Percentage

What was the most common favourite food?

Our bodies need food to grow healthily - check out pages 92 and 93 of the *Book of Wonders* to discover more!

Who provides most of your food?
How about going to say "thank you"?!

Sometimes people say grace before eating to say thank you to God. In the Bible, there are lots of examples of people thanking God for looking after them and giving them everything they need. Here's one:

"Give thanks to the Lord because he is good.
His love continues for ever.
Give thanks to the God of gods.
His love continues for ever.
Give thanks to the Lord of lords.
His love continues for ever."

Psalm 136:1-3 (NCV)

What might you say thank you to God for?

INTELLIGENCE

We're all intelligent, right? We've all got skills in all sorts of stuff. Perhaps you've got good body control (see page 10), an ear for music (see page 24) or are a star baker (see page 20). Our brains process the information around us and in our memories to help us navigate the world and picture things in our minds.

How good are you at working out spatial puzzles? Try out these two! You will need: paper, scissors, a pencil.

Place your paper over these shapes. Trace around them and then cut them out. Then try to rearrange them into a square! Once you've solved the puzzle, stick it into this book.

A TANGRAM

This puzzle is thought to have been invented during the Chinese Song dynasty (an empire that ruled much of China from AD 960 to 1279).

Professor John Wyatt works at University College London. He says: "An astronomer born in 1571 once said when talking about his work, 'I was merely thinking God's thoughts after him.' Our mind follows God's mind (we are made in God's image). We can use science to find out about God's wonderful creation and also use things like medicine to bring healing and renewal."

Isn't it great that we can use our intelligence to discover and enjoy all kinds of different things about God's wonderful universe?

THE HABERDASHER'S PROBLEM

This was invented in 1907 by a mathematician called Henry Dudeney.

These pieces can make both a square and a triangle. Can you make both?

Can you design any of your own puzzles like these? Make them out of card and challenge your friends!

Stuck? Why not search online for the answers!

THE POWER ALL AROUND YOU!

Your house is probably full of items that use electricity. Go on a hunt to see how many you can find. Draw some of them here – make sure you stay safe!

Inside your house.

What do they all do? If you needed to cut down on the electricity you used, which ones could you do without?

We get lots of our electricity by burning fossil fuels in big power stations. We can help look after God's world by using less electricity. If we're careful with what we turn on and when, then we will use less fossil fuel and release less CO_2 and other gases into the atmosphere. If you have the *Book of Wonders*, check out pages 49, 80 and 81 to find out more.

MAKE A POTATO BATTERY

You will need: a voltmeter, a copper coin, a galvanised (or zinc-coated) nail, two alligator clips, a large potato and a small bulb (ask your parent or carer to help you get hold of all of these - tell them to check out the note to parents on page 2).

Push the nail into the potato. Do the same with the copper coin. Make sure the coin and the nail aren't touching.

Connect the red lead of the voltmeter to the coin using an alligator clip. Connect the black lead to the nail using the other clip.

The voltmeter should show the voltage running through the circuit you have just created.

0.93

You can create a chain of two or three potatoes to produce enough electricity to power a low-voltage LED clock or a bulb!

ACID OR ALKALI?

Inside your house.

God's amazing universe is made up of all kinds of different chemicals with lots of different properties. Scientists use the pH scale to show how acidic or alkaline they are. If chemicals are very acidic their pH value is low (0 to 3); if they are very alkaline, the value is high (12 to 14). If something is neither acidic nor alkaline, is described as neutral and has a pH value of 7.

There are a lot of things in your house that contain chemicals which make them acid or alkali. Some of them you should leave alone – they're too acidic or alkaline (such as toilet cleaner or chlorine bleach) and you shouldn't touch them because they can hurt or damage your skin. But there are some things you can test!

YOU WILL NEED:

Vinegar
Lemon juice
Tap water
Fizzy bottled water
Milk
Washing-up liquid
A tomato
Bicarbonate of soda (mixed with water)
Bowls
Litmus paper

(Ask your parent or carer to help you get hold of all of these and some other things that are safe to test.)

Put a little bit of your different substances into different bowls. Test each one by dipping a piece of litmus paper into it (or pressing the paper onto it). Litmus paper changes colour according to how acidic or alkaline a substance is. Compare the colour with the chart on the opposite page. This will show you the pH value.

Write down your results in this chart:

Substance	pH value

Which substance was most acidic? Which was the most alkaline?

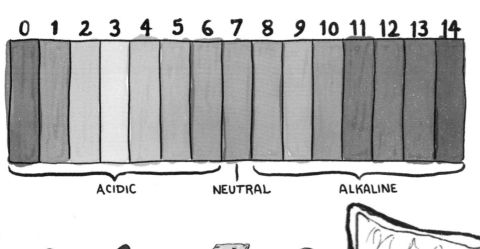

0 1 2 3 4 5 6 7 8 9 10 11 12 13 14

ACIDIC   NEUTRAL   ALKALINE

DAILY BREAD

Bread is often called a "staple food" — that means it's an essential basic food. Yeast is an important ingredient in making bread rise, to make a big and fluffy loaf like the ones you can buy in the shops.

But did you know that yeast is a member of the fungus kingdom? You can find out all about fungi on page 58 of the *Book of Wonders*.

Here's how to make a loaf of bread.

YOU WILL NEED:

7 g dried fast action yeast
1 tbsp sugar
300 ml warm water
1 tbsp vegetable oil
500 g strong bread flour
1 tsp salt

1. Mix the sugar and yeast together in the warm water and leave for 10 minutes, until a brown froth forms on the surface of the water (this means the yeast is alive and working hard!). Then stir in the vegetable oil.

2. Mix together the flour and salt. Pour in the yeast mixture and mix everything together until you get a soft dough.

3. Tip the dough out onto a clean surface (if the dough is very sticky, then dust the surface with some flour first). Knead the dough for about 5 or 10 minutes. You can do this by squishing the dough back and forth on the surface with your hands.

By kneading, you develop the gluten in the flour. Glutens are a group of proteins found in cereals. They help foods keep their shape and stick together. The more you knead, the stretchier the gluten gets, giving a softer, more elastic dough, which means it can trap more bubbles later on, leading to a light, fluffy bread once baked.

4. Lightly oil a large bowl and put the dough in it. Cover with cling film or a tea towel and leave for an hour until the dough grows to twice its original size.

Once activated by the warm water, the yeast feeds on the sugar, releasing carbon dioxide. This creates more and more bubbles in the stretchy dough. The bubbles make it light and fluffy and the ball of dough grows in size!

5. After an hour, tip the dough out of the bowl and squash it down, so that all the carbon dioxide bubbles burst. Form the dough into a shape (a loaf or small rolls) and place on a baking sheet. Leave for 30 minutes to rest and plump up (the yeast carries on releasing carbon dioxide making your dough even fluffier). Then bake for 30 minutes (for a loaf) or 15-20 minutes (for rolls) in a preheated oven (180 °C).

You can make types of bread using bicarbonate of soda and buttermilk instead of yeast. The acidic buttermilk reacts with the alkaline bicarbonate of soda to give off carbon dioxide. You don't need to knead the dough or leave it to grow in size.

If you don't eat wheat or gluten, look online to find a good gluten-free bread recipe. There are lots to try - why not bake two or three and see which is the best?

Bread is yummy and important. For lots of people, it is their main food. In John's story of Jesus in the Bible, Jesus describes himself as the "bread of life". What do you think he meant by that? Read John chapter 6 to find out more!

MESSAGE IN A BOTTLE?

Communication is really important to people, no matter where we live or what language we speak. There are lots of different ways to communicate (and have been lots of others throughout history). Why not have a go at some of these different methods?

Flag semaphore is a way of communicating over distance using flags. Can you send a message to a friend using semaphore? Grab some flags and find out!

SEMAPHORE ALPHABET

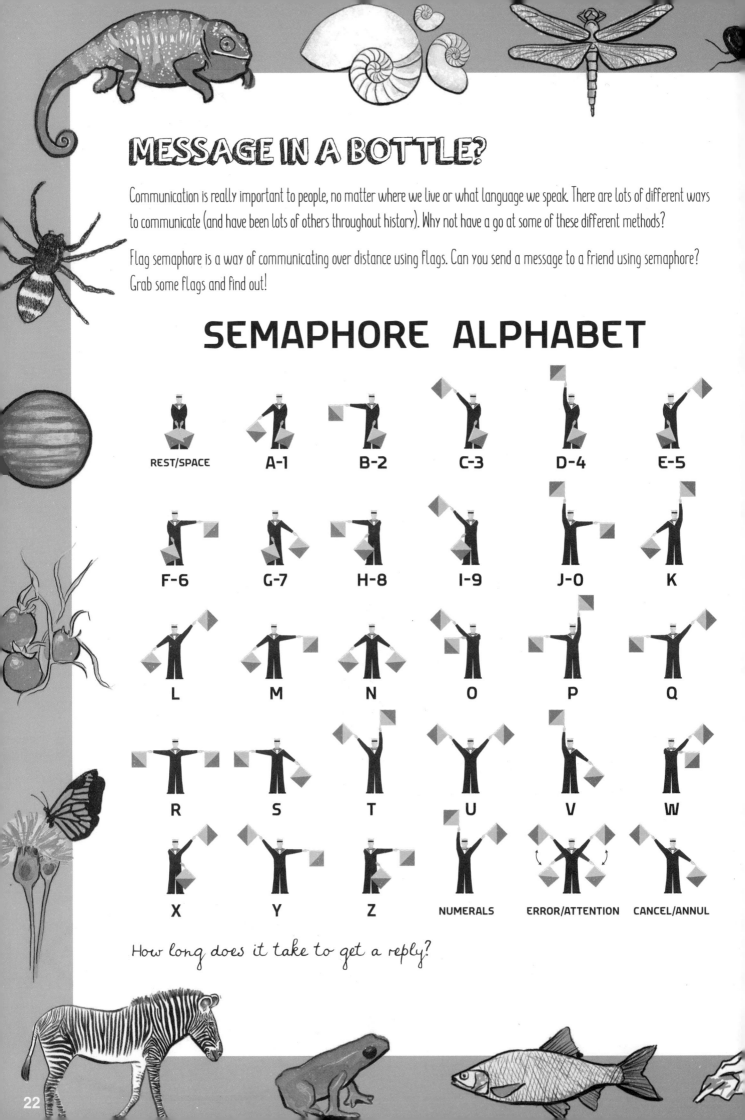

REST/SPACE   A-1   B-2   C-3   D-4   E-5

F-6   G-7   H-8   I-9   J-0   K

L   M   N   O   P   Q

R   S   T   U   V   W

X   Y   Z   NUMERALS   ERROR/ATTENTION   CANCEL/ANNUL

How long does it take to get a reply?

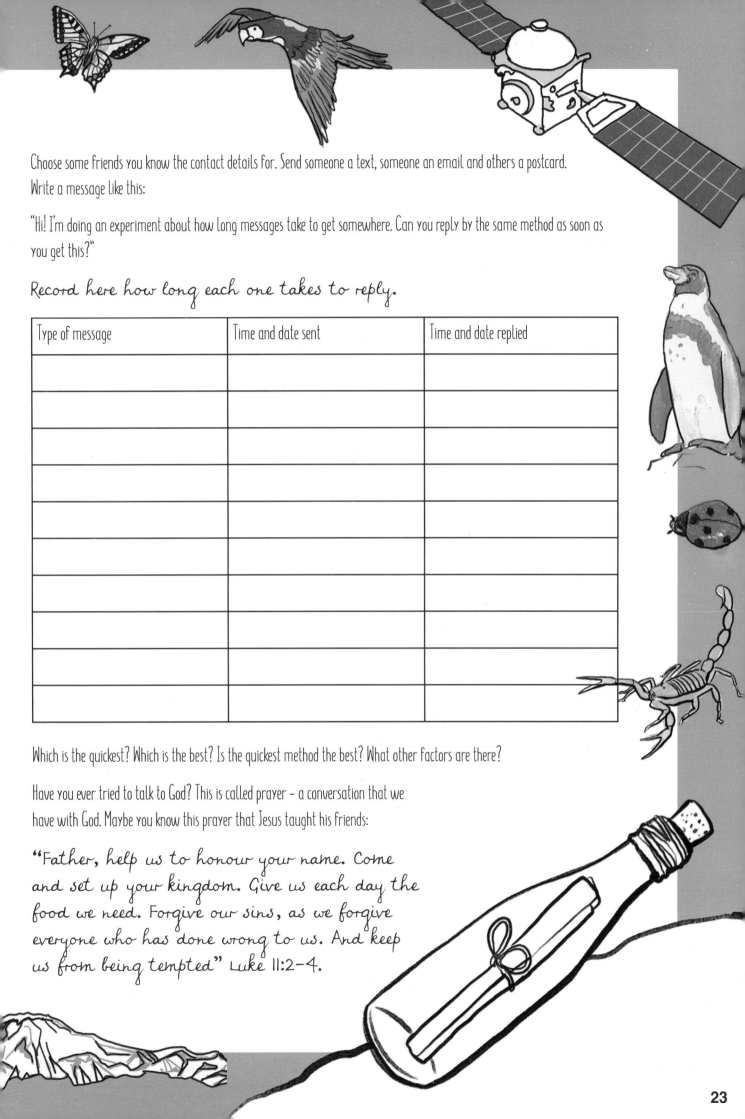

Choose some friends you know the contact details for. Send someone a text, someone an email and others a postcard. Write a message like this:

"Hi! I'm doing an experiment about how long messages take to get somewhere. Can you reply by the same method as soon as you get this?"

Record here how long each one takes to reply.

Type of message	Time and date sent	Time and date replied

Which is the quickest? Which is the best? Is the quickest method the best? What other factors are there?

Have you ever tried to talk to God? This is called prayer – a conversation that we have with God. Maybe you know this prayer that Jesus taught his friends:

"Father, help us to honour your name. Come and set up your kingdom. Give us each day the food we need. Forgive our sins, as we forgive everyone who has done wrong to us. And keep us from being tempted" Luke 11:2–4.

MAKING MUSIC

Do you play an instrument? What is it? How does it make a sound? Or do you sing? Check out how soundwaves travel and how your ear receives those vibrations in the *Book of Wonders* (pages 42 to 45).

DRAW A DIAGRAM OF YOUR INSTRUMENT HERE, OR LOOK IN A MIRROR AND DRAW A SELF-PORTRAIT OF YOU SINGING!

PLAY YOUR INSTRUMENT AND TRY TO WORK OUT HOW IT MAKES A SOUND. IS IT ONE OF THESE?

CLARINET

As you blow, the end of the reed vibrates, sending soundwaves down the body of the clarinet. You change the note by closing or releasing the keys.

PIANO

When you hit the keys, hammers in the piano strike strings to make vibrations. The shorter the string, the higher the note.

VIOLIN

The vibrations in a violin are made when you drag the bow along the string. The vibrations echo inside the body of the violin and amplify the sound. Putting fingers in different places on the strings makes them longer or shorter. The shorter the string, the higher the note.

VOICE

Your vocal cords are folds of muscle tissue in your throat. They vibrate together as you breathe to create a sound – this is how we speak and sing.

24

HERE'S THE FINAL SONG IN THE BOOK OF PSALMS IN THE BIBLE (PSALM 150):

Shout praises to the Lord!
Praise God in his temple.
Praise him in heaven,
his mighty fortress.
Praise our God!
His deeds are wonderful,
too marvellous to describe.
Praise God with trumpets
and all kinds of harps.
Praise him with tambourines
and dancing,
with stringed instruments
and woodwinds.
Praise God with cymbals,
with clashing cymbals.
Let every living creature
praise the Lord.
Shout praises to the Lord!

You can use the body and mind God has made to play your instrument, and get really good at it! Does anything of what you've discovered in the *Book of Wonders* or this activity book make you want to play your instrument or sing because of how amazing God is? Maybe you could write your own song about God and all the wonderful things he does?

ABOUT MY NEIGHBOURHOOD

What do you know about the area you live in? Draw a map of your neighbourhood here. Make sure you include your house, your friends' houses and your favourite places to hang out and play. In addition to all the landmarks, parks and shops, mark on anything of scientific interest, such as electricity substations, nature reserves, canals or recycling centres.

What things about your neighbourhood are amazing or beautiful?
What would you like to change?

You have the power to make changes in our world. Perhaps you could write a letter to your MP or local council thanking them for the things you like about your neighbourhood and asking them to change some of the things you would like to be different.

Jesus said that the most important things we could do were to love God and love other people (he said that in Matthew 22:37-39). What do you think about that? How easy is it to love the people who live around us, or go to our school?

How easy is it to love God?

BUILD A BRIDGE

Are there different bridges in your neighbourhood? Why not find one and draw it here?

Like the arch on pages 102 and 103 of the *Book of Wonders*, bridges direct the pressure of their weight down columns – different bridges do this in different ways. Here are some kinds of bridges; which kind is the one you've drawn?

ARCH BRIDGE

BEAM BRIDGE

SUSPENSION BRIDGE

TRUSS BRIDGE

CANTILEVER BRIDGE

Can you make your own bridge?

YOU WILL NEED:

Paper straws
Sticky tape or masking tape
String
A pile of coins

1. Have a look at the different kinds of bridges (you might want to check some of them out online to find out more) and then try to build a bridge that will hold some coins. Triangles are a very strong shape (truss and cantilever bridges are made from triangles).

2. Once you have made your bridge, pile coins onto the middle. How many can you pile on before the bridge collapses? What kinds of changes can you make to improve your bridge?

Why not make different kinds of bridges and see which is the strongest? Draw your constructions here and record how many coins they were able to support.

To build a bridge you need to make sure you have really solid foundations, you have to look for the right spot, dig down deep to get rid of the muck and get right down to the solid rock, then dig in deep and start to build. The Bible says our lives are a bit like this, it tells us they are stronger and better when we build them on the solid rock of Jesus.

BIRD SURVEY

Birds are amazing! Check out pages 60–61 in the *Book of Wonders* for wonderful facts about brilliant birds. Do you have a favourite?

What kinds of birds can you see in your local park? Get a parent or carer to take you and write down all the different types on this chart. Draw a picture, if you can, and count how many of each one you can see.

Bird	Picture	How many

Which bird is the most common in your neighbourhood?

If you don't know what a bird is called, use the RSPB's "Identify a bird" tool (www.rspb.org.uk)!

Thinking about birds can show us some of the amazing variety of God's creation. He cares for the birds, and he cares for you too. Here's what Jesus says about birds and us!

"I tell you not to worry about your life. Don't worry about having something to eat, drink, or wear. Isn't life more than food or clothing? Look at the birds in the sky! They don't plant or harvest. They don't even store grain in barns. Yet your Father in heaven takes care of them. Aren't you worth more than birds?" Matthew 6:25,26.

God loves all his creation - that includes birds, and us! What do you want to say to God about this?

THE CLOUDS IN THE SKY

Clouds might just look like fluffy cotton wool stuck in the sky, but they're important and wonderful. There are lots of different kinds of clouds in the sky. What can you see now?

CIRRUS

CIRROCUMULUS

CIRROSTRATUS

ALTOCUMULUS

ALTOSTRATUS

STRATOCUMULUS

NIMBOSTRATUS

CUMULUS

CUMULONIMBUS

STRATUS

Look through your window at the same time every day and mark on this page the different types of clouds you can see. Use a different colour of pen for each day. How many different clouds can you see in a week?

SUNDAY	
MONDAY	
TUESDAY	
WEDNESDAY	
THURSDAY	
FRIDAY	
SATURDAY	

For a different view, go with a parent or carer to the top of a hill or somewhere else high up. What can you see?

God's friend, David, wrote a lot about how awesome God is. Even the clouds are a brilliant creation!

"He covers the heavens with clouds; he prepares rain for the earth; he makes grass grow on the hills" Psalm 147:8.

YOUR VERY OWN WEATHER STATION

Weather is fascinating - we talk about it all the time! Check out pages 36 and 37 of the *Book of Wonders* to find out more. Here's how to make your very own weather station, so that you can keep an eye on what's happening in your neighbourhood!

RAIN GAUGE

YOU WILL NEED:

A clean jar, masking tape, a marker pen, a ruler

1. Stick a length of masking tape vertically to your jar.
   Use a ruler to mark centimetres and half centimetres on the tape.

2. Place the gauge outside and check how many centimetres of rain falls each day or week.

BAROMETER

YOU WILL NEED:

A round balloon, a clean jar, rubber bands, a paper straw, a toothpick, sticky tape, a glue stick, a piece of card, a marker pen

1. Cut the end off the balloon (just below where the round bit starts) and stretch the balloon over the mouth of the jar. Use rubber bands to secure the balloon and make it airtight. Tape the toothpick to one end of the straw. Put glue on the other end of the straw and stick it to the balloon.

2. On the card, write 'High' at the top and 'Low' at the bottom. Place it behind the jar, so that the toothpick sits in the middle of the high-low scale. Mark a starting position on the card where the toothpick is pointing.

3. When air pressure is low, the pressure in the jar will be greater and will push the balloon up, making the toothpick move downwards. When air pressure is high, the pressure in the jar will be lower and will pull the balloon down, making the toothpick move upwards. Mark on the card where the pressure is each day.

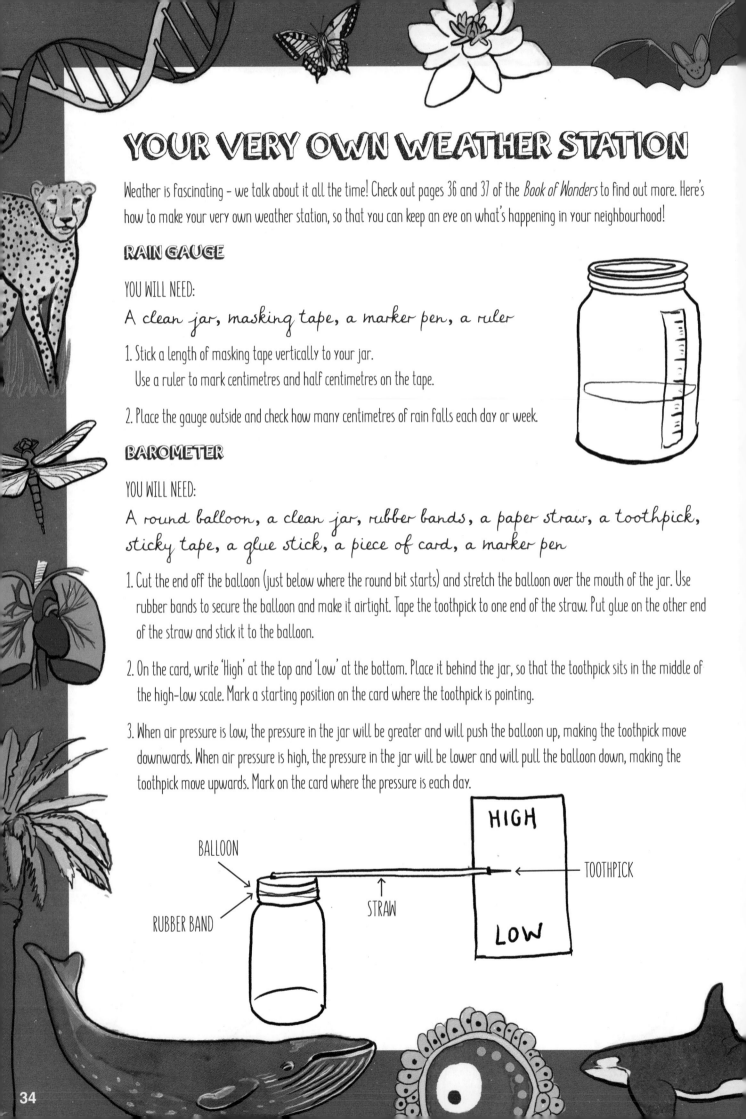

BALLOON

RUBBER BAND

STRAW

HIGH

LOW

TOOTHPICK

WIND VANE

YOU WILL NEED:

A lump of clay (or Plasticine or play dough)
A pencil with an eraser on the end
A paper straw
An arrow shape cut out of paper
Sticky tape, a straight pin
(like the ones used in sewing)

1. Push the pencil into the lump of clay with the eraser end pointing upwards. Tape the arrow to one end of the straw. Push the pin through the midpoint of the straw and then down into the pencil eraser. Leave it loose enough so that the straw can spin around.

2. Place the wind vane outside and keep track of in which direction the wind is blowing.

Did you know the New Testament part of the Bible was written in Greek? When the Holy Spirit is talked about, the Greek word *pneuma (say "noo-ma")* is used; *pneuma* also means wind. Like the wind, the Holy Spirit is everywhere. We may not be able to see the Holy Spirit but we can see the difference he makes - just as we can with the wind!

You could also place a thermometer outside to keep track of how hot it is!

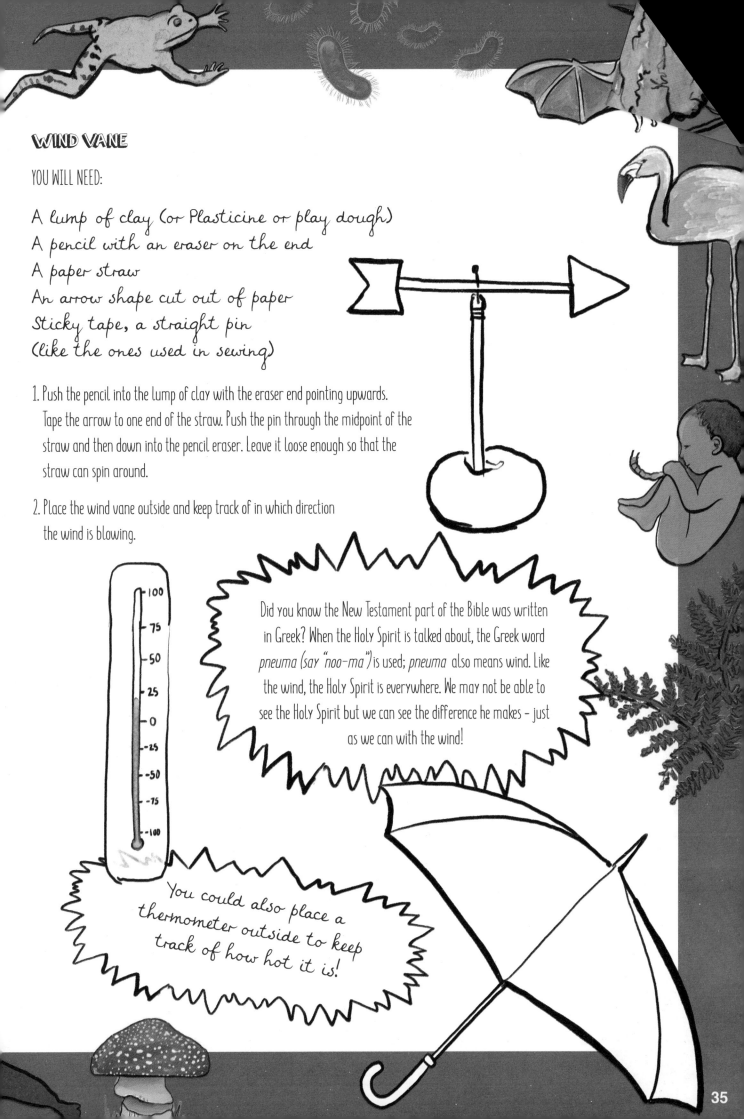

SACRED SPACES

Are there any places in your neighbourhood where people go to meet together and worship God? Architects have been designing church buildings for many years, to provide special spaces for people to talk to God, sing to him and listen to what he says. Some of these buildings are very old and some are very new. They might look different. Can you find a local church and draw the outside of it here?

Can you see anything special about the church building? Do you think it's there to be decorative, to help it stand up, or both? You might see:

TOWERS

FLYING BUTTRESSES

COLUMNS

All of these things were used on big old buildings to help them stay up!

If you can go inside the church, look for signs of what might hold the church up and draw them here.

Check out pages 102 and 103 of the *Book of Wonders* to get some clues!

Architects think a lot about windows and lighting. That's because the way a building is lit is important for how people feel in the space and what the building is used for. How does light get into your local church? Look at the windows – what shape and colour are they? If it's cloudy during your visit what do you think they would look like on a sunny day? Draw one here:

Have you ever experienced a church service? What was it like? Which bits did you enjoy? How did it make you feel? If you haven't, talk to your parent or person who looks after you – perhaps you could find a local service you could go to?

How does light get into your house or your school?

MINIBEAST HUNT

There are some amazing tiny creatures around us in God's wonderful creation! You can discover more about them in pages 76 and 77 of the *Book of Wonders*. Why not go on your own minibeast hunt? Take this book with you to a park, wood or piece of open ground and see what minibeasts you can find (make sure you get permission from the people who look after you first). You could also keep a note of how often you find certain creatures. How many woodlice or ants can you see? Can you find a centipede?

DRAW WHAT YOU FIND HERE!

Hunt carefully for minibeasts so as not to hurt them. If you pick one up, always put it back where you found it.

Look under rocks and piles of leaves – lots of minibeasts hide out there – but be careful that you don't disturb their homes. If you're near a pond, lake or river, you might also see damselflies and dragonflies – more information is on pages 66 and 67 of the *Book of Wonders*.

Be careful near ponds, lakes and rivers – they can seem very beautiful but be quite dangerous!

DRAW WHAT YOU FIND HERE!

Which minibeast is your favourite? Isn't it amazing that God created such tiny creatures and made them so complex and interesting?

LOVELY LEAVES

When you're out and about in your neighbourhood, you'll probably find lots of trees, but what kind are they? Horse chestnut or beech, sycamore or larch? Find some leaves and draw them here or stick them in! (Don't pull leaves off trees, wait till they fall to the ground. You might need to wait until autumn.)

Can you find these leaves?

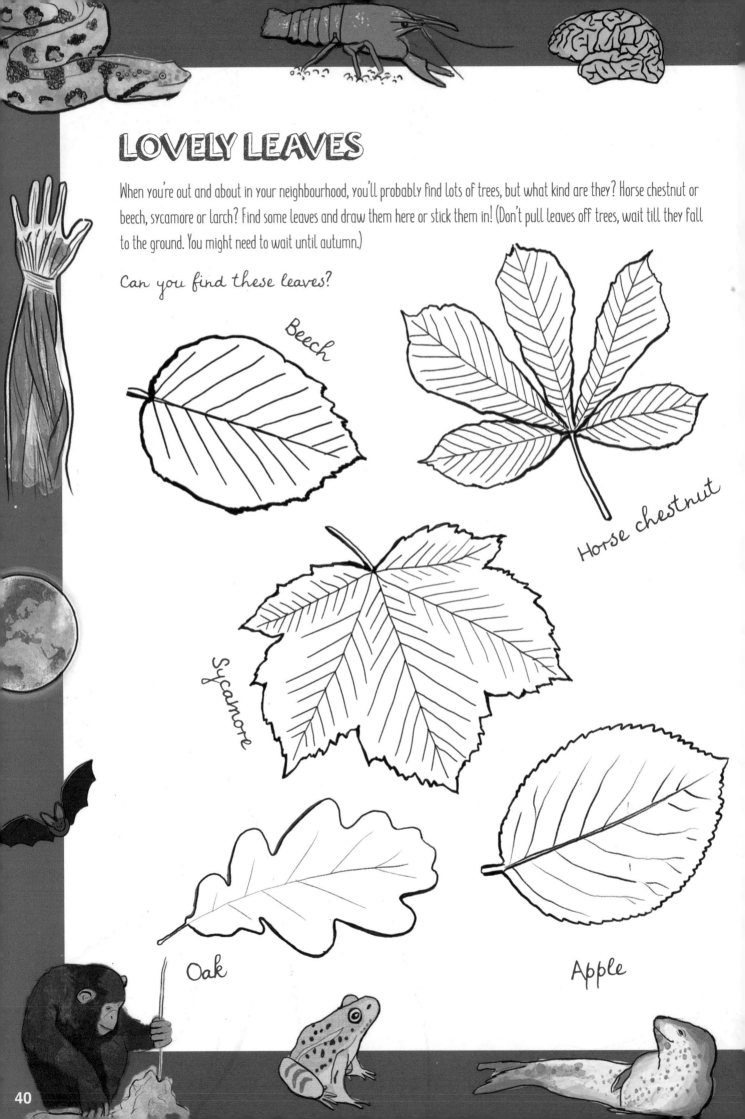

Beech

Horse chestnut

Sycamore

Oak

Apple

Find a leaf and turn it over. Place it behind this page and gently colour over it with a crayon. You should get an image of the leaf. Can you see the veins? These transport water and minerals, as well as food energy. Find out more on pages 54 and 55 of the *Book of Wonders*.

If you need help identifying trees, the Woodland Trust has an app you can use! Go to www.woodlandtrust.org.uk.

God really loves all of his creation. The Bible is full of verses that talk about trees, using them as examples to help us understand things like how we can grow well when we are 'rooted' in God's love (such as Jeremiah 17 and Psalm 1). The Bible also talks about how the trees worship God by just being the way he created them to be. God thinks trees are wonderful! And the more we learn about them, the more we get to share in that joy!

THE PATTERN OF YOUR NEIGHBOURHOOD

What patterns can you see in nature around you?
Find some patterns and draw them here.

What about a spider's web? A cauliflower? The sand on the beach?
A wasps' nest?

Which is your favourite?

(Be careful around wasps' nests - don't disturb the wasps!)

The writer of this psalm – a poem written to God – tells us:

"Our Lord, by your wisdom you made so many things; the whole earth is covered with your living creatures" Psalm 104:24.

The writer thinks that the beauty of creation tells us about God. What do these beautiful patterns tell you about God? Why not write your own poem about the patterns all around you and what you want to say to God about them?

ABOUT MY WORLD

The planet we live on is full of wonders. Using the *Book of Wonders* and other things that you know, fill this map with some of the amazing things in the world – deserts, volcanoes, waterfalls, glaciers, coral reefs and canyons. Don't forget to include where you live!

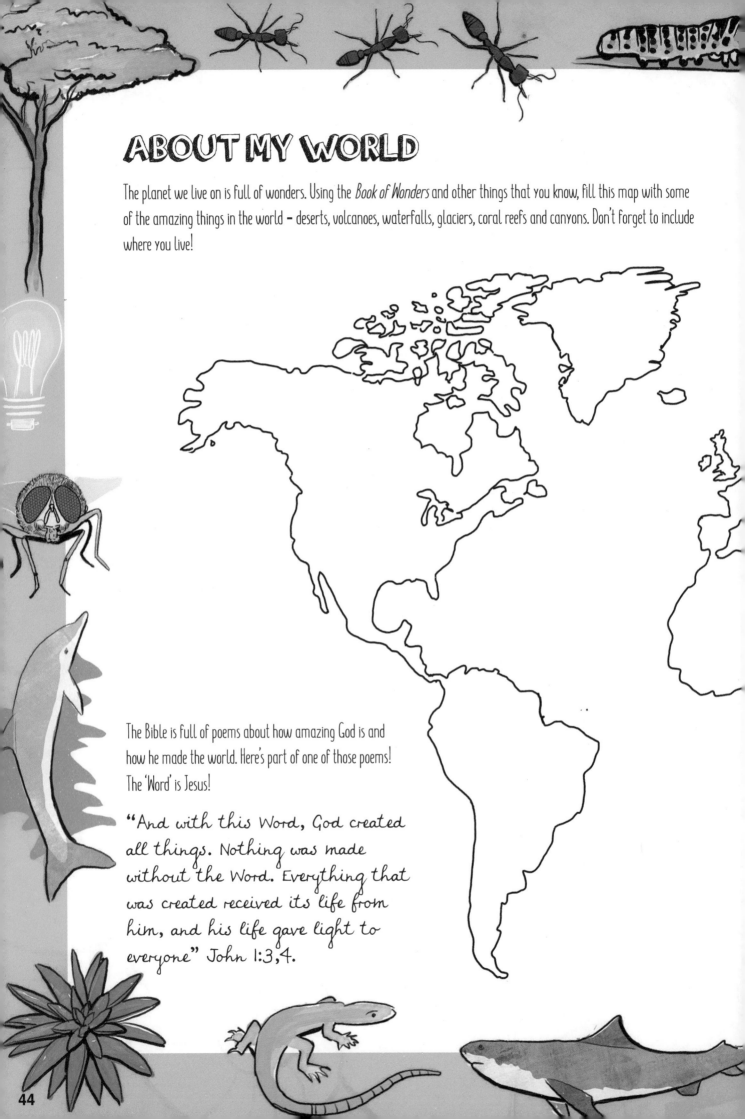

The Bible is full of poems about how amazing God is and how he made the world. Here's part of one of those poems! The 'Word' is Jesus!

"And with this Word, God created all things. Nothing was made without the Word. Everything that was created received its life from him, and his life gave light to everyone" John 1:3,4.

"God holds the deepest part of the earth in his hands, and the mountain peaks belong to him. The ocean is the Lord's because he made it, and with his own hands he formed the dry land" Psalm 95:4,5.

What do these verses tell you about God? Do you have any questions you want to ask God?

ERUPTION!

Volcanoes are all around the world, from Eyjafjallajökull (say "EY-yah-FYAT-la-yer-KUH-tel") in Iceland to Mount Fuji in Japan, from Mount Etna in Sicily to Mount St Helens in the USA, from Mauna Loa in Hawaii to Krakatoa in Indonesia. They can cause damage, but they are also amazingly powerful and important for our world. They form new islands and create areas where lots of plants grow. (Check out pages 26 and 27 of the *Book of Wonders* for more about volcanoes.)

You can make your own volcano! You'll need some help from an adult, but it's a great project to try out.

TO MAKE YOUR MOUNTAIN, YOU WILL NEED:
A big cardboard square
(cut from a large box)
An empty fizzy drink bottle
Strips of cardboard
Sticky tape or masking tape
Strips of newspaper
PVA glue
Paint and paintbrushes

Use some tape to secure the bottle to the middle of the cardboard square. Stick strips of cardboard from the neck of the bottle to the edge of the big square. Go all the way around the square until you have a rough mountain shape. (Make sure you keep the top of the bottle open.) Stick strips of newspaper to the mountain shape with PVA glue, overlapping them as you go. If you want a sturdier mountain, stick on lots of layers of newspaper (letting each layer dry before applying a new one).

TO MAKE YOUR VOLCANO ERUPT, YOU WILL NEED:

Warm water
Washing-up liquid
Red or orange food colouring
Bicarbonate of soda
Vinegar
Measuring jug and spoons
An old jug

Put a tablespoon of water, a squirt of washing-up liquid , a tablespoon of bicarbonate of soda and a splash of food colouring into a jug and mix together. Pour into the bottle in the middle of your mountain. Measure out about 80 ml of vinegar and pour that into the bottle. Watch your volcano erupt!

The vinegar (an acid) reacts with the bicarbonate of soda (an alkali) and foams up. The washing-up liquid traps the gas to create more bubbles, and the food colouring makes it look like lava!

The writers of the Bible saw volcanoes as a sign of God's power. This is what one writer thought:

"You look at the earth, and it trembles. You touch the mountains, and smoke goes up"
Psalm 104:32.

Volcanoes are amazingly powerful and important for our world. They form new islands and create areas where lots of plants grow. But they can also cause damage. Check out page 26 of the *Book of Wonders* for an idea of how a Christian makes sense of the destruction caused by volcanoes.

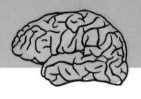

MAKE A DAM

Dams are constructions that stop a river flowing. In the natural world, they are sometimes built by beavers, who make their homes in them. Humans make them to form reservoirs used as supplies of water or to make hydroelectric power. Some of them are huge! Search on the internet for some large dams and mark them on the map on pages 44 and 45.

HOW ABOUT MAKING YOUR OWN DAM?

You'll need some adult help with this, but why not get your friends to help you too?

1. Find a little stream you can play safely in and look for some building materials; you'll need things like rocks and sticks.

2. Choose your spot – start with a narrow stretch so that it won't take too long.

3. Start from the bottom and work up. You might need to plug holes with smaller stones, sand or leaves. Remember, use materials you find on the ground – don't pull leaves or branches off trees. And don't use any plastics or other materials made by humans – you don't want to add to the plastic pollution in the oceans.

4. Can you see how the water starts to back up behind your dam? Can you see anything getting trapped in your dam? Any fish? How is the water reacting? Is it trickling through the dam, is it swirling and swooshing or has it been completely stopped by your work?

Draw your dam here. Also draw anything you can see in the water caught behind your dam. Draw what has happened to the water trapped in the dam.

Once you've finished, make sure you take down your dam. Enjoy dismantling your dam and restoring the stream to its natural course!

If you're at the beach, you could dam up some of the tidal streams that are created when the tide goes in and out.

In the book of Job in the Bible (Job 38:8-11), God uses word pictures to talk to Job about his power over the oceans and waters:

"When the ocean was born, I set its boundaries and wrapped it in blankets of thickest fog. Then I built a wall around it, locked the gates, and said, 'Your powerful waves stop here! They can go no farther.'"

Just as you set a boundary with your dam, God is in charge of the oceans!

Jesus showed he had power over the waters – check out Luke 8:22-25 to find out more.

49

ENDANGERED CREATURES

The world God has made is filled with fabulous animals. But sadly, the activities of humans have caused many species to become endangered. Some are close to dying out altogether. Find out about one such creature and fill this page with drawings and facts about that animal!

WHALE SHARK

TIGER

Discover more at the International Union for Conservation of Nature and Natural Resources' Red List of Threatened Species website: www.iucnredlist.org.

JACKRABBIT

LEAF CHAMELEON

Success! The red kite was almost extinct in the wild in Britain, but it was saved by one of the world's longest-running protection programmes. It has now been successfully re-introduced to England and Scotland, and made a significant recovery in Wales.

The Bible says God has given us the responsibility to look after the world:

"God said, 'Now we will make humans, and they will be like us. We will let them rule the fish, the birds, and all other living creatures'"
Genesis 1:26.

"Rule" doesn't mean we can do just what we like! God loves our planet and we can help take care of it. What can you do to look after creation?

LIGHT TO GROW

We all need light to grow! Humans need sunlight – our bodies make vitamin D from direct sunlight on our skin (vitamin D is essential for healthy bones). Plants need light to grow, too. Do this experiment to find out how important light is!

YOU WILL NEED:
Large sheets of black paper
Sticky tape
Scissors
Three identical plant pots or yogurt pots
Cotton wool
Cress or mustard seeds
Water

1. Fold a sheet of paper in half and stick two of the edges down, leaving one of the shorter ends open. This should give you a large paper envelope. Do this with another sheet of paper but, this time, cut a window in one side of the envelope.

2. Put the same amount of cotton wool in the bottom of each plant pot. Place the same number of seeds on top of the cotton wool in each pot. Then moisten the cotton wool in each pot with a teaspoon of water.

3. Put the pots in a sunny place – outside in a garden or on a window ledge. Cover one pot with the window envelope and another with the envelope with no window. Leave one pot uncovered.

WHEN DOING AN EXPERIMENT LIKE THIS, IT'S IMPORTANT TO KEEP EVERYTHING (APART FROM THE ONE THING YOU'RE CHANGING ON PURPOSE) THE SAME FOR EACH EXAMPLE! OTHERWISE YOU DON'T GET RELIABLE RESULTS.

Leave the pots alone for a week and then remove the envelopes. How have the seeds grown in the three different environments? DRAW YOUR RESULTS HERE!

OPEN

WINDOW
ENVELOPE

FULL
ENVELOPE

What does this tell you about light? What effect does light have on plant growth?

The Bible talks about Jesus being the light of the world (in John 1:1-5,9 and 8:12). What do you think that means? How can someone be light for the world? Do the results of your experiment help you answer that question?

THE COLOURS OF LIGHT

Do you ever think about light having a colour? Light usually looks clear or white to us, but it's actually made up of different colours. The different colours come from different parts of the light having different "wavelengths". All together, they make up a "spectrum". Find out more on pages 38 and 39 of the *Book of Wonders*. We see the different colours when the light is "split up". You can do this yourself by making something called a spectroscope! (You might want to ask an adult to help you to gather all the materials you need for this.)

YOU WILL NEED:

A shoebox
A pen
A ruler
A protractor
Scissors
A square of aluminium foil
Sticky tape
A piece of diffraction grating
(a slide or cut from a sheet, both are available online)

15°

2 CM

1. Draw a line on the top of the box from one short side to the other. The line should be about 2 cm from one of the long sides. Using the protractor, measure an angle of 15° from one end of the line. Draw another line across the box to mark out that angle.

2. At the pointy end of the angle, cut a 1 cm square hole in the side of the box. At the other end, cut a 2 cm square hole in the side of the box below the 15° line.

3. Tape a 6 cm square piece of aluminium foil over the hole at the pointy end. Cut a narrow vertical slit in the foil, centred on the hole.

4. At the other end, tape a piece of diffraction grating over the hole, on the inside of the box.

5. Look through the slit and you should see the different colours of the spectrum of light. (If you don't, you might need to rotate the diffraction grating 90° and then stick it down again.)

Use pencil crayons or felt-tip pens to draw the colours you can see!

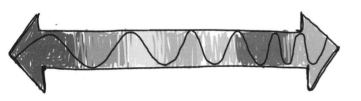

RED HAS THE LONGEST WAVELENGTH AND VIOLET THE SHORTEST.

What do you think when you see a rainbow?
Do you know what Christians think about?
A promise from God! Check out
Genesis 9:12-16 in the Bible
to find out more.

ABOUT THE UNIVERSE

God's universe is enormous! We've been able to use science to find out some really cool stuff about it! Scientists estimate that there are around one hundred billion galaxies in the observable universe. Our own galaxy, the Milky Way, is 105,700 light years across, and it has a black hole at the centre. It is a barred spiral galaxy.

What do you know about the universe? Fill this space with drawings of different galaxies and facts that you find out about our universe! Here are a few to start you off...

A light year is the distance that light travels in a vacuum in one year (that's about 9.46 trillion kilometres).

The most distant galaxy we can see with a telescope is called GN-z11. It's 32 billion light years away.

The Andromeda Galaxy is our nearest neighbour. It is 2.5 million light years away.

We're not sure what 85% of the matter of the universe is. Scientists think there is something called Dark Matter, but exactly what this is still an exciting mystery!

The name "galaxy" comes from the Greek word γαλαξίας (say gal-ak-SEE-us) meaning "milky".

When you think about the vastness of the universe, how do you feel? What words would you use to describe the universe?

What does the vastness of the universe tell you about God? Here's what David, a friend of God, thought about:

"I often think of the heavens your hands have made, and of the moon and stars you put in place. Then I ask, 'Why do you care about us humans? Why are you concerned for us weaklings?'" (Psalm 8:3,4)

God cares about the universe and God cares about you!

THE EARTH, SUN AND MOON

The Earth, like all the other planets in the solar system, orbits around the Sun. The solar system is amazing, and we can use science to learn more about it, including the way that the earth, sun and moon move through space!

Every day the Earth spins all the way round (rotates) on its axis. That means that the part of the Earth we are on sometimes directly faces the Sun (daytime) and sometimes faces away from the Sun (night-time). From where we are, that makes it look as though the Sun moves across the sky from east to west every day. We can use a sundial to track the Sun's "movement" across the sky and work out the time of day!

YOU WILL NEED:

A paper plate
A lump of play dough
A long pen or a stick (such as a chopstick)
A marker pen
A sunny day!

1. Check out the weather forecast and find out if it's going to be sunny all day.

2. Put a lump of play dough in the centre of the plate and stick your large pen or stick upright in the dough.

3. Place the plate outside in the sun (weight it down if it's windy!) and mark where the shadow of the pen or stick falls.

4. Write the time next to that mark. Come back every hour during the day and mark where the shadow falls (and write the time).

5. At the end of the day, you'll have a record of the Earth's rotation. Mark where the plate is on the floor so you can put it back in the same place in the future.

This is how sundials work to show the time – on future sunny days, place the plate (still with the pen or stick stuck in the dough) in the same place. You'll be able to tell the time by where the shadow falls.

While the Earth is rotating on its axis, and orbiting the Sun, the Moon is orbiting the Earth too. As the Moon goes around the Earth, the light from the Sun we see reflected by the Moon's surface changes, depending on where it is in its orbit. The Moon we see seems to grow from new moon to full moon and back again. Let's find out how.

YOU WILL NEED:
A torch
A tennis ball
A ping-pong ball
Jaffa Cakes or other soft, round biscuits

1. Turn the torch on and place the tennis ball on a table or on the floor. This is the Earth. Place the ping-pong ball (the Moon) in between the torch (the Sun) and the Earth. This is a new moon: the light from the Sun is hitting the side of the moon we can't see from the Earth. So we only see the dark side. To us it looks like there's no moon at all!

2. Move the Moon anticlockwise a quarter of the way around the Earth. This is called a half moon (or quarter moon, since we're actually only seeing a quarter of the sphere of the Moon). Half the Moon is lit up, as seen from the Earth. Move the Moon another quarter around the Earth. Now the Moon appears fully lit up – this is a full moon. As you move further around the Earth, the light we can see reflected by the Moon shrinks again.

3. Take four biscuits. Can you eat enough of each biscuit to show how much of the light we can see from the Earth at each quarter rotation? Now take four more biscuits and try to fill in the gaps between each quarter orbit – can you find out the names for these different phases of the Moon?

The Moon has been a useful measure for people for many years. In the Bible, the people of God used the Moon to mark the time and hold their festivals:

"Sound the trumpets and start the New Moon Festival. We must also celebrate when the moon is full" Psalm 81:3.

How does the orbit of the Moon affect our lives?

PICK A PLANET

Which planet in our solar system is your favourite? Use this page to write or draw all about it! You can look at pages 20 and 21 of the *Book of Wonders* to get started.

Choose a planet and draw what the planet's surface or atmosphere looks like. Then fill the space around it with any rings and moons that it has.

Find out facts about the planet and write or draw those in. What have scientists done to find out about it? What spacecrafts have visited the planet? How long is a day or a year there? What's the temperature? What's the weather? Is there any air? Would you like to go there? What would be different from Earth?

Astrophysicist Dr Althea Wilkinson studies the planets and the stars. She says: "I feel awe and wonder at what I see in the universe. The more I see these huge, enormous things and the vast timescales, the more I get an appreciation of who God really is. God's not an old man sitting up on a cloud. God's the one who created everything."

BUILD A ROCKET

Did you know you can build your own rocket? You might not reach your favourite planet (see pages 60 and 61), but it should get airborne!

YOU WILL NEED:

A camera film canister (available online)
Antacid or vitamin tablets
(fizzing ones such as Alka Seltzer)
Water
Safety goggles
Outside space
An adult to help

1. Take the top off the canister and put one teaspoon of water in the bottom.

2. Go outside and put your safety goggles on. Snap a fizzing tablet in half. Drop the half-tablet in the canister and snap the lid on very quickly. (It needs to be tightly shut, so you might need an adult to help you.)

3. Turn the canister upside-down (so that the lid is on the floor) and retreat to a safe distance. After around ten seconds, the cannister will fly into the air with a pop! (If the rocket doesn't pop, then wait at least 30 seconds before going back to it.)

When the water touches the antacid tablet, it starts to dissolve it, giving off carbon dioxide. The carbon dioxide gas builds up in the canister until the pressure is so great that it blasts the canister into the air! If the rocket doesn't work, the cap probably isn't on properly, allowing the gas to escape.

CHECK OUT PAGES 14 AND 15 OF THE BOOK OF WONDERS FOR MORE RADICAL REACTIONS!

You could add extra bits onto your canister (such as fins made of card or extra decoration) to see if they improve the flight of the rocket! Try adding more or less water or fizzing tablets, or breaking the tablets up into more small pieces.

You could try this several times, and estimate which "flight" goes the highest. Do any of your extra add-ons improve the flight? Why do you think that is? Record all your findings here.

Rocket/ Launch number	Modifications	Height reached

We might think of rockets that make it all the way into space as being some of the most powerful things there are. In your rocket the carbon dioxide builds up and gives the rocket power to fly. In the Bible, Jesus is described as having great power. But Jesus' power doesn't come from carbon dioxide. Grab a Bible and find the story of Jesus and the army officer in Luke 7:1-10. What does this tell you about Jesus' power?

THE STARS IN THE SKY

What can you see in the night sky? The next dark evening when there are no clouds, go outside (get a parent or carer to come with you, if you need to) and look up into the sky.

What can you see? The adult with you might be able to download a stargazing app. If they can, use that to identify the stars and planets that might be above your head. Remember that Mercury, Venus, Mars, Jupiter and Saturn are all visible without the aid of binoculars. However, if you have binoculars or a telescope, you'll be able to see things a bit more clearly.

Draw what you can see here:

WHAT ARE YOUR FAVOURITE CONSTELLATIONS?

God's friend David wrote a lot about how amazing God's creation is. In a song about God (called a psalm), he sang all about God creating the skies!

"He decided how many stars there would be in the sky and gave each one a name" Psalm 147:4.

YOUR VERY OWN COMET

Comets are lumps of ice and rock that career around the universe. We know about some of the ones that shoot through our solar system (and out into our galaxy). Some are regular visitors: Halley's Comet travels past the Earth every 75 years. It was last seen in 1986 and should reappear in 2061. It can be seen on the Bayeux Tapestry, as it appeared in the sky in 1066 when William the Conqueror invaded England.

COMET

DUST TAIL

COMA

HEAD

NUCLEUS

ION (GAS) TAIL

The comet is made up of a solid "nucleus". This is surrounded by a "coma", a cloud of gas and dust coming off the nucleus. It has two tails: an ion (gas) tail and a dust tail.

MAKE YOUR OWN COMET!

YOU WILL NEED:

Kitchen foil
Three colours of ribbon
A chopstick
Bamboo skewer or length of garden dowelling

1. Cut long lengths of two colours of ribbon (these are the gas and dust tails). Cut much shorter lengths of the third colour to represent the coma.

2. Scrunch a piece of kitchen foil securely around the end of your long stick, then tie all the long pieces of ribbon around that ball of foil, making sure all the ends of the ribbon can flow freely.

3. Wrap more kitchen foil around the ball, holding the ribbon out of the way so that it doesn't get tangled up.

4. Once you're happy with the size of the nucleus, tie the shorter lengths of ribbon around the ball and fan the ends out so that they surround the nucleus (like the comet in the diagram).

5. Wave the comet around and the tails should flow out behind it!

Comets travel far and wide, and are only very small compared to the vastness of the universe. Their journeys are lonely ones, but God knows all about them. The Bible tells us that God delights in all his creation. He knows all about you and cares for you too. What does that make you feel? What do you want to say to God?

WRITE A PSALM

In the Bible, the writers of the book called Psalms loved to write poems and songs to God, saying how amazing he is. They looked at themselves, the world all around them and the universe itself and were inspired by the wonders of God's creation. Check these verses out:

"You are the one who put me together inside my mother's body, and I praise you because of the wonderful way you created me. Everything you do is marvellous! Of this I have no doubt"

Psalm 139:13,14.

"In the beginning, Lord, you laid the earth's foundation and created the heavens"

PSALM 102:25.

"People far away marvel at your fearsome deeds, and all who live under the sun celebrate and sing because of you. You take care of the earth and send rain to help the soil grow all kinds of crops. Your rivers never run dry, and you prepare the earth to produce much grain"

PSALM 65:8,9.

When you read the *Book of Wonders* and try out the activities in the *Book of Wonders: Activity Book*, what do you want to say to God?

Why not write your own song or poem to or about God here? Decorate it with all the different things you have learnt about in *Book of Wonders: Activity Book.*

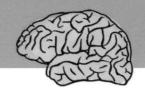

WHAT GOD HAS DONE

God has done some amazing things! All through the *Book of Wonders: Activity Book*, you've been discovering all sorts of things about the world around you. Have you discovered:

- THE TASTE TEST (PAGES 12 AND 13)?

- THE FUNGUS IN BREAD (PAGES 20 AND 21)?

- THE VARIETY OF BIRDS IN YOUR NEIGHBOURHOOD (PAGES 30 AND 31)?

- THE VOLCANO EXPERIMENT (PAGES 46 AND 47)?

- THE SPECTRUM OF LIGHT (PAGES 54 AND 55)?

- YOU FAVOURITE PLANET (PAGES 60 AND 61)?

However, the *Book of Wonders: Activity Book* is not only about the world around you. It's also about the you that your eyes can't see – your spirit. The pages are full of examples of God's great creation and how it all works. God set in motion and sustains everything that exists (including the things we haven't discovered yet), but he wants to know you too.

David was a friend of God who wrote some songs that appear in the Bible. He was amazed that God who made the universe would be interested in him. You might have read this on page 57, but here it is again:

> "I often think of the heavens
> your hands have made,
> and of the moon and stars
> you put in place.
> Then I ask, 'Why do you care
> about us humans?
> Why are you concerned
> for us weaklings?'"
>
> Psalm 8:3,4

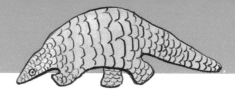

But God does care! He cares so much about us. We often make mistakes, from the way we treat the planet, to the decisions we make in daily life (check out pages 78–81 of the *Book of Wonders*). God wants to be our friend, but these things that we do wrong can get in the way. So God sent his Son Jesus to Earth. He did some amazing things (see pages 34 and 88 of the *Book of Wonders*).

Jesus came to take away everything that separated us from God, so we could be his friends again. Even though he did nothing wrong, Jesus took the blame for all the wrong things people in the world have done – past, present and future. Jesus won against the darkness by living a perfect life, dying and coming back to life again! Now all we have to do is trust in Jesus and we can be friends with God who made the whole universe!

YOU MIGHT WANT TO SAY THIS PRAYER:

Dear God,
Thank you for making this amazing universe and everything in it, including me!
Please help me discover more about you and how I can get to know you better.
Amen

A man called John wrote all about Jesus in the Bible. In John's story of Jesus, you can read this:

"God loved the people of this world so much that he gave his only Son, so that everyone who has faith in him will have eternal life and never really die"
John 3:16.

WHAT DO YOU THINK?